messy but magical

Hannah Collman

BookLeaf Publishing

Presentation by *BookLeaf Publishing*

Web: www.bookleafpub.com

E-mail: info@bookleafpub.com

ISBN: 9789357440684

First edition 2023

one for weirdlings

The Ghost

I wasn't always this way
I'm surprised that you,
someone in view,
can even hear the words I say

You hear but cannot see,
and that's the opposite
of how it used to be

All I wanted
was to be wanted
around

For some sorry reason
I thought best not make
a sound

They can't hate a creature of quietness
For on what foundation would they have to base
a judgement?
I was a wallflower in likeness;
observing and patient and smiling in
contentment

The ache of being interrupted or ignored soon
resigned
once I took a non-verbal vow
and grew to love my ability to fade from the
conscious mind

It was becoming quickly clear I was invisible to
many
I heard the sharing of stories and tales though
my ears weren't invited to any
I saw the sorrow in the smilers, the weakness in
the strong,
those oblivious to obvious answers that had been
there all along
And so it would seem, this silent life was
proving,
you can learn a lot when you practice the art of
listening more often than mouth moving.

But don't worry, your secrets are safe with me
For I am a ghost, after all,
and only the 'crazy' people talk to those they
cannot see.

Sunflower Rock

Field blanketed in yellow
reminds me of you
A glow in the sky
painted bright blue
A gentle breeze
blows through my hair
So if you please,
meet me right there:
Where the sunflowers dance
and grass is green
The peaceful atmosphere
like something of a dream
Keep it secret, keep it locked
Where we groove out
to the sunflower rock

Masquerading

Dance with me through dissolution
Take my hand and show me how to be
All I long for is inclusion,
and for someone to find a friend in me
Tell me which mask you prefer,
I will wear it whenever we meet
Please be patient as we ponder
for in this dance, I may step on your feet

Walk confidently, but wander...

I question why we're ashamed to daydream
To let your imagination fly away
and attention float down a silver stream
of careful carelessness

There's so much to life
yet we choose to focus on so little
Let our feet stand still
and our courage grow brittle

I'm tired of confinement,
being cornered into conforming,
when all I want to do is watch the butterflies
flutter by
gracefully performing

I've always had an inquisitive mind,
with a curious nature,
but an understanding of this
few succeeded to ever capture

"The girl who is in her own little world."
"Away with the fairies,

or some place beyond."
Some say her ways would forever be frowned
upon

For a while I was led to believe that all I was
was a weirdling,
doing a bad thing,
despite the joy, to me, it would bring

But as I grew older
I began to lead myself…
Down a path where I was free to ponder
and so, from that world, I will sunder

Into a tranquil place
where I walk confidently,
                              but wonder…

Bug friends

Excuse me, stag beetle
You're going the wrong way
Would you mind
if I helped you find
where it is you're heading, today?

Bumble bee, how do you do?
You're looking slightly drained
Some sugary water
I think it is oughta
get you feeling right as rain

My apologies, wiggly worm
I nearly didn't see you there
Let me move you out of sight
of any birdies who might
be looking for tasty grubs to share

Hello there, human
I see you're helping the bugs too
If you agree there's no feeling greater
than having a friend in nature
then you've got a friend in me, too.

a positive puzzle

People talk about their missing peice
but I feel like the puzzle's complete,
and I'm just a spare,
that doesn't fit in anywhere
I don't feel mad, or as I've been wronged
It's more like I'm in a box to which I don't
belong

I may never be the favourite,
and that is entirely okay
I'll always be an oddball,
doing things their own way
To most I've been forgettable
and never allowed my say
For too long I've been dismissed
but I'll make them proud someday

Clutter bug

I am a clutter bug
I like to collect
An enthusiast of useful things
which haven't yet found their use

Trinkets and lockets,
tokens and pockets,
of keepsakes of memories made

Bits o' ribbon and buttons,
newspaper cuttings,
souvenirs and 'something's saved

This and that, bric-a-brac,
an unusual ornamental cat,
…A hoarder, some might say

But I say this is my collection:
of divine finds
and a superior selection
featuring lots of lovely things

If you were to laugh and ask
"What do you need so many shells for?"
I couldn't reply with why,

but it'd only make me love them more

Home to a plush toy population
A floor of garments and dresses
Boxes and bags of bits and bobs
Yes, it all makes many a messes

Vases, pots, and pretty glass bottles
These are my mementoes
Things I feel could be useful,
so why wouldn't I hold onto those?

In a world of disposal
and things too often discarded
I take great pride
in being resourceful and guarded

So please be kind to my clutter
Though it seems, in neglect, I retreated
I am happy to still have things I hold dearly
Plus, you never know when you might need it!

Keep on sailing, sailors

Keep on sailing, sailors
Trudging through the night
Round foggy bog bend
To show our foes we will fight
'Til the bitter end

All aboard to our destinies
Lives lost for the chance to live
Yet they took more than what they had to give
For in war, there are no victories

The moon shone brightly that night
And on their lifeless faces, reflected the light
Of that crystal globe, under which they
Fought and fell
Now only history knows,
So time will have to tell

How those sailors kept on sailing
Trudging through the night
On foggy bog bend
To share with their foes,
Their brutal bitter end

New Development

New
Development

Oh trees of tall,
you must not be fooled;
Please don't fall for the axe

Though its handle of wood
makes you think that you should,
one must never trust the lumberjacks

See how they mark you with an 'X'?
They did the same to all of your friends,
and I fear soon they'll be plastered everywhere

I've seen it before- the branches go first,
Animals evicted, roots are lifted; it'll only get
worse.
For the forest we all loved will too soon be
completely bare

Just so
a block
of flats
can be
built there.

I like you, spider

I am so very sorry about that
Humans can be quite loud, can't they?
Not to worry, you're safe now
I'll keep you out of harm's way

The window ledge can be your corner,
to do with whatever you wish to
It's just nice to have some company,
I'm so very glad her slipper missed you

I know you never meant any fuss
You were probably just cold outside,
Well, I like you, spider
and you're welcome here anytime

I saw a face in my coffee cup

I saw you there
Tuesday last
Late morning
Meek day
Sorry coffee
Quarter past

The cafe crowded
Noise of clinking cups
Milk steam screams
People talk
Chairs clang
Workers washing up

But I couldn't hear it
May as well be unaware
Because I saw you
Again, I know,
I know I saw you there

In the froth
and powdery chocolate dust
Your face,
I know,
I saw it,

I just know, I know, I must

And then you were gone
Suddenly subsided
But I caught you
in my coffee cup
You were,
Please, you can't deny it

You won't talk, though, will you?
What about Wednesday 28th?
The cloud
Until I rubbed my eyes
That was you
I'm certain I saw your face

And so many other times;
Like in the lake or in the linen
The seeded loaf's mould growth
The countless carpet stains,
and that's only the beginning

You're right, something's started…
And yes, I'm scared of what it could be
I can't rub my eyes on this one
I'm scared, but not of you,
Of me

Hermit Crab

There once was a little crab
who was mostly merry
but often times drab
she couldn't find her place in this ocean wide

Whilst other crabs were crabbing,
getting to work,
pinching things, and nabbing,
she'd struggle socially, sitting by the seaside

She wasn't necessarily crabby;
When with crustacean peers
she was actually quite happy,
but she just couldn't wait to be taken by the tide

It was troubling to understand
"Why am I not like the others?
I feel my safest buried in the sand"
It upset set her so, and so, alone, she often cried

But there was something she lack
See, she wasn't just a crab;
A shell should be on her back -
Her own safe place to resort to and reside

For she is a hermit crab
and that is ok
It's not something bad
Folks will see she just needs time to heal and
hide

Restored

Enlighten me with loveliness
Don't leave me for the grave
Though my body grew cold and lifeless
There's still a chance I'll be saved

Restore my broken parts
Then I'll repair you in return
Place me propped, warm by a fire
We can watch the woodchip burn

Healing

Nature is a wonder
Working upon my broken skin

I am in awe of the process
And how quickly healing begins

The fibres of my garment
Sticking to my flesh

Like a bird gathering oddities
For padding out her nest

My body, a patchwork blanket
Telling tales of where I've been

I am forever thankful, body
For these scars protected what's within

Home-grown Hope

I used to be bitter
but now I'm better
Time winds by
each 365 feels faster than the last
And thus must hold tightly of the reins
Steering into that promising place
where adventure awaits.
In the pit of pre and past experience
there lies a merge of all things felt;
I have found new beginings
Slowly, losses I have healed,
a scattering shower of broken glass,
shards of sorrow brushed aside
In tidy piles
in crowded corners
cast asunder,
Burden's bridges burnt
A fire ignited inspires new growth,
or so they say,
Replemish the soil,
nourish the soul
Growth is not a race-
Some seeds seek solitude,
and if solitude is due,
then do be so,

If so, then so be it
Climb at your own pace
Time is for the taking
and the taking will suffice
For it is yours to do with what you please
I no longer live in awe of the light,
but embody a glow myself
From fabrication, I no long borrow
Though now wish to share,
I harbour a hope for each new morrow

Ghost at the Pelicon Crossing

Stopped still in the passenger seat
Back, far left
Rain trickling down the window
Night drawing in
Moon shine bouncing off the dampened streets
The glare of red reflecting

Taxi driver agitated
What for is not so clear
But he says
"Stupid lights,
they're always playing up like this."

The light at the pelicon crossing is red
But how was the button ever pressed?
There is no one there to be seen
Well, not to the human eye,
At least.

The Faerie Phase

Once again, the faerie phase
indicates a trouble change
Field seams frost like lace,
soaking up the sunny rays
of a bright winter morning haze
Fresh feeling on my face
Oh, what a wonder,
What a delight,
And one does wonder
If you will accompany me
To the forest fire dance, tonight?

I am where I am wonderful

You may look upon me unkindly,
as though I am the one who is troubled
As if fading from this farcical place is such a
pity
My eyes may glaze
over an expressionless face
Reserving motion for where I am mentally
For I am not there anymore;
I am where the fairies dance
I am by the waterfall of sparkling silk
I am lavished in lemongrass
My face painted a picture of content
I watch floating fungal spores
And listen to the troll bridge's snores
I spend my days in a rose-tinted haze
Where there are summer flowers in bloom
On a carpet of autumnal leaves
Scents of spring surrounding me
And that refreshing frost of winter on my face
Where the rain tastes of lemon drops
And snow, warm cotton balls and candy floss
The elves of the elements love me here
They bathe my soul in sanctuary,
conserving and caring for my spirit
I am at peace with myself and everyone else

I am in a place far from there
A place many dream to venture but very few
dare
I am where the trees tickle the sky
And the wind whistles in shimmers of silver
So should you ever ask of her fate,
the girl in your world with the glazed-over face,
I laid her to rest, not killed her-

For she fought long enough in that world of
yours,
And found it unkindly and deeply troubled to the
core.

The Other Side

Growing exhausted of what seemed like
an uphill battle, chasing the light
at the end of a tunnel
A tunnel which bridged over my happy place
forever being pulled back
or was the light being pulled forward,
further away,
always out of reach
Never could I quite make it, never would I be
free
All I had was my echo for company
But that light was my life
and my guiding force to fight
So you fight back the faintness
Go into an automated mode, all becomes a blur
But we were built to survive and keep on
keeping on,
or so I've heard

Suddenly it seems I'm at the start again
No wait, I'm on the other side somehow
Looking back- I did it. I made it to the end
So where do I go to now?

what I know to be true

Then all at once, life is simple,
offering a variety of reasons to live for
There is harmony in your heart
and a gratitude for the hurt
You were never really a mess
despite the forest fires and the shipwrecks

When all was lost and falling apart
your broken pieces became a work of art
Take off your mask and don't be afraid
You are a marvel, and mustn't be tamed
Secure with a ribbon the memories kept
You befriended the demons so hard to accept

Walk with your past but don't hold hands
Remember your roots when your branches
expand
You can still hug your teddies and talk to the
fairies
Still see signs when it appears there aren't any
Say hello to the bugs who brightened your day
Recognise the ones who loved you all of the way

You may even find you grieve the pain
sometimes

because it was a constant in which you could
confide
So much so, you grew to love what you loathed
but it was a blur and a burden, as you now know

This is an experience from which many will
learn
Rising from the flames as they lavishly burned
You are not a ghost, you are a living legend
Your strength still built when destruction
beckoned
Pity those who have a taste for unkindness
and cutting down others who may differ in
likeness

This is, so far, what I know to be true
I finally found my euphoria,
And have great faith, that you will find yours,
too.

How now, canal?

How now, canal?
Any boats been by?
The river rippling
Tickly tides, low rise
Reeds bobbing along
Water wavering, whistling
The most gentlest of songs
People pattering down the bank
Wind blows the rushes reaching
The swans swimming past
how now, canal?
You are at peace,
at last.